Is There a Hell for Children?
A Spiritual Guide for Parents & Children

Is There a Hell for Children?
A Spiritual Guide for Parents & Children

Jacquelyn D. Currie

Printed in the United States of America
First Edition April 2010
Visit our website at www.jacquelyndcurrie.com

10 9 8 7 6 5 4 3 2

Delo Publishing Group
541 Moline Road
Memphis, TN 38109

Library of Congress Cataloging-in-Publication Data

ISBN: 978-0-615-36257-1

Dedication

I dedicate this book first to God for giving me the inspiration to write this book and to thank him for being a part of my life every day. I also want to dedicate this book to all of my seven grandchildren, my sister Patricia, my 'play sister Mattie,' and especially my son-in-law Larry and daughter Tasha.

Special dedications to my son, Howard – do not play, get right with God and you will do well in life.

To my son, Kerwin...ditto and I love you all so much.

To my Mom, Delores G. Johnson, you made it all possible. Without you there would be no me.

Acknowledgments

Thank you Lord again and again. I can't thank you enough for inspiring me to write this book.

Shelia E. Lipsey, our paths have crossed over and over again. Thank you from the bottom of my heart for your help and guidance.

My brother-in-law, Rasheed Akbar, for your artistic talent.

Special thanks to my brother, Earl Johnson, and Kamilah Lea-Webb.

Table of Contents

Encourage Yourself

Introduction

Everyday while I am at work, one way or another, news comes up in a discussion. I rarely contribute because I seldom watch the news unless it is Breaking News. It is depressing to hear that most of the news that is reported is about some type of serious, heinous crime being committed. What is so disturbing about the discussions at work is how many of these stories concern children committing these heinous crimes. Furthermore, the rate of truancy has escalated at our schools, and the crimes committed by children are horrific crimes that were committed one time by only adults.

In the not so distant past, crimes our youths committed were associated with petty crimes. Sadly, in the 21st century we see a huge increase of heinous, serious, and violent crimes being carried out by young people. The system seems to have become lax because nowadays children can not only get their hands on guns, but they carry them into the schools and kill other children and staff.

Some people find it to be a form of entertainment to watch and video fights between children and in turn post them on the internet where they are sensationalized even more.

One evening, I decided to watch the news. I listened and watched the report about three young men at a local high school that cut school and went on a robbing spree all over the city. The high school coach from the school was interviewed. He said that the young men who allegedly carried out this crime spree were all good students; one of the young men had a four year scholarship to attend college. After watching the news that night, my spirit hit me so hard that I cried out to the Lord and asked, "Lord, do these children know they can go to hell for all the wrong they are doing?" Thus, the decision was made for me to write *Is There a Hell for Children?*

I want parents and children to know that it is time to grow closer to God, and reinforce in our children the consequences of their actions.

Jacquelyn D. Currie

Chapter 1
Family Structure

Married with children, single with children, blended families, no matter how the family is made up it is still a family. The common thread of the family is parenting. Parenting is definitely not easy; it is a huge responsibility.

From the beginning of life, a child's character is molded. This is the early development phase of a child's life where the child is solely dependent on the parent. The window to instill in them right from wrong is from birth to kindergarten. The word of God says, "Train up a child in the way he should go and when he is old he will not depart from it" (Proverbs 22:6 C.E.V.).

In the early development stage, children have their own personalities and their own emotions. As parents, by example, guidance and instruction, the words *yes* and *no* are introduced.

Children learn in phases. It is not an overnight process. All children have their own level of learning.

Today many families are faced with difficult children. There are some children who challenge the authority of their parents. They act out in unacceptable ways and are just plain out of control. Every day is a test of situations that occur when raising children. "Do not fail to correct your children. You will not kill them by being firm and it may even save their lives" (Proverbs 23:13-14 C.E.V.).

It is a parent's responsibility to nurture a child's behavior by showing and teaching them the difference between right and wrong. Preparing children for life requires great discipline on the parts of parents.

To be good parents, there are tools needed in raising children. Parents should make a practice of exercising patience, being consistent, and responsible, and have values and morals. The most valuable tool is introducing God and Jesus to the home, planting a spiritual seed that can be nurtured, watered, and thereby allows the child to grow spiritually.

Parents must be careful when it comes to what children are being exposed to. Children take their cue from their parents. Parents, You must strive to live Godly lives. This is the main purpose of your being. "Good people live right and God bless the children who follow their example" (Proverbs 20:7 C.E.V.).

As parents, you are responsible for setting examples of how you want your children to be. With so much chaos going on today in the world, you must make time and keep a handle on your children.

As parents, you should know who your children's friends are, where they hangout, and watch and observe them in the home. It is mainly at the home front where enforcement of steering your children on the correct path begins. "All children are foolish, but firm correction will make them change" (Proverbs 22:15 C.E.V.). You should not send your children out in the world if instructing them is not taught at home. "Raise them properly. Teach them and instruct them about the Lord" (Ephesians 6:2-4 C.E.V.).

Through creation, we are all God's children, adults and children alike.

Children do not have the maturity in the early years of their life. Children are dependent on their parents to supply them with the guidance needed to become a valuable part of this world. Through experience, along with time, children develop characteristics in phases of their learning range of knowledge and understanding. As parents, and only with God's help, can you expect to raise Godly children.

Parents, strive to live a Godly life by being a mentor and setting good examples for yourselves and your families. When you set good examples, you in turn want your children to display good behavior, respect, love and wisdom.

Today we live in a high tech society. Constant, healthy communication in the home is extremely important. We communicate using several devices such as the landline telephone, cellular phone, text messaging, computers, social media networks and e-mail. The main human element in communicating is simply plain talking. Talking is an avenue to express what is on one's mind. For some reason, expression of speech is somewhat difficult in what we say face to face.

In any relationship, communication is very important in expressing, understanding, and having a two-sided conversation. When rearing children, talking is an essential and necessary component to establish that line of communication, reassurance, creativity, and developing a relationship.

Listening is another facet of communicating. Listening is an art that has to be developed over a period of time. We all have selective hearing. We hear what we want to hear. When it comes to children, we have to use plain language so guidelines and rules established in the home can be followed. This will aide in establishing a comfort zone of trust with your children.

Keep the lines of communication open. You should listen, observe, and use Godly wisdom when you are instructing children. Problems can be caused when the lines of communication shut down.

Lack of proper communication between parents and children, can lead kids to seek other alternatives when they feel they are being misunderstood or not heard. This is really a form of rebelling. Children may find themselves caught up in situations that they cannot handle. This is one of many reasons why parent communication is a key component, starting with the early phase of rearing children.

Maintain an open door policy in the home. Make yourself available when children have problems. Children need the assurance of love and trust by and from their parents. Love conquers all. Children will develop a sense of relying on their parents and most likely will not shield or keep things within themselves.

Chapter 2
Show and Tell

There are numerous factors that contribute to a child's development. The best way is through example and by repetition. It is an investment of being committed and dedicated incorporated with instructing.

Being a parent takes special skills. There is no formal training involved. Preparation of being a good parent is having the patience, the strength, and the endurance. Raising children is a full-time job. "Be patient when you are being corrected! This is how God treats His children. Do not all parents correct their children? God corrects all of his children, and if He doesn't correct you, then you do not really belong to Him" (Hebrews 12:7-8 C.E.V.).

The early phase of a child's life is what I call the show and tell stage. It is this stage where examples and explanations are used to instruct and guide the child. It is being the best possible example in how you display yourself as a parent when training your children. Every child is different. There is no 100% perfect method for raising a child. It is through trial and error that parents teach their children to grow as productive adults in today's society. The roller coaster ride begins.

I admit that being a parent can be overwhelming at times. There will be ups and downs, disappointments, mistakes, but there are also bountiful rewards of parenthood. Some children learn the easy way and some learn the hard way. This is where patience and repetition comes along with a lot of love.

Children develop many traits. Sometimes children take on the characteristics they see being displayed by their primary caretaker(s). The way you talk, laugh, and your lifestyle in the home does not go unnoticed by children. Children see and hear everything.

Children are people. Children will display and act out their emotions. As parents, you tell and show them about their behavior. When teaching children, they focus on the parent's behavior. Children soak everything in like a sponge. They pay attention to vocabulary, anger behavior displayed, drinking, mode of dress, and the type of people parents choose to surround themselves with around their children.

As parents, you have a responsibility to correct unacceptable behavior of your children. "Teach your children right from wrong, and when they are grown they will do right" (Proverbs 22:6 C.E.V.). The standards set are standards developed by the child. It comes down to lifestyle.

Some children will challenge their parents. It's about who is in control. Love and discipline go hand in hand. "If you love your children, you will correct them, if you do not love them, you will not correct them" (Proverbs 13:24 C.E.V.).

There are parents who want to be good parents, parents who do not know how to be parents, and parents who do not want to be parents. Parents, you have a moral obligation to be the best parents you can be when children are brought into this world.

Children are helpless and solely dependent on their parents, as you should be solely dependent on God for all of your needs. God should be your source to call upon and as caretakers of your children; you need to instill in them and not deprive them of the benefits derived from being raised in a Christian home.

Parents, you have a moral obligation to protect, guide, discipline, and steer your children properly in the ways the Lord instructs you to live your lives. You must consistently show and teach your children about love, values, and responsibility.

So, ask yourself if you are setting your children up to travel the correct path of life. What happens if you fail to raise your children in the logic of learning, discipline and seeing that their needs are met? The answer is better answered in Proverbs 24:10 which says, "Do not give up and be helpless in times of trouble" (C.E.V.).

As parents, you have to believe that with a firm hand, and by leaning and depending on God that you can raise children who will grow into mature adults that will be able to function successfully throughout life's situations.

The book of James speaks on faith and wisdom. It states, "But you must learn to endure everything, so that you will be completely mature and not lacking in anything. If any of you need wisdom, you should ask God, and it will be given to you. God is generous and will not correct you for asking." (James 1 vs. 4-5 C.E.V.). If ever you're in doubt, or not sure that you are getting through to your child, pray and ask the Lord.

Chapter 3
Are You Sending Your Children to Hell?

In a perfect world, children would be obedient, get all A's on their report cards, grow up to be great adults and raise wonderful children. In a perfect world, a parent's life would be trouble free. There would be no worries of their children experiencing exposure to violence, drugs, gangs, and confused about what gender they are. But this is not a perfect world, and unfortunately that means there will be imperfect situations. The best that parents can do is to love and nurture their children and do what is best for them.

Where does Hell fit into the equation of rearing a child? Please understand that without proper wisdom, love, discipline, values, responsibilities, and exposure to God and Jesus, children can be led down a path that no parent wants to face. Add to this equation, **blinded by love parents**, **protective parents**, **do right parents**, and **do nothing parents** and see how the formula unfolds.

Blinded by love parents close their eyes, block out, and excuse their child's behavior. This is not helping the child to cope with the realities of life. You see these children screaming and throwing tantrums. They are labeled as spoiled brats that need a firm hand to steer them properly. As the child grows older, understanding consequences of the stuff they get themselves into has no bearing. Their mindset tells them, 'my parents will fix it.' These children have no understanding of the word *no*.

Protective parents shield, will not let go, and hold their children back. This hurts the children as they may not have the significant tools needed when dealing with everyday life. This may give them a lack of confidence when making important decisions and might cause them to become unsure of themselves because the parent has always made the decisions for the child.

Do right parents know what their child may be capable of and will do whatever it takes to steer their child right. The parent is observant, attentive to changes, and instills in the child the consequences of their actions. You see these children learning from their mistakes and understanding that their parents have their best interest at heart.

The **do nothing parents** allow their child to hang with bad friends, will let their child sell drugs, and some do nothing parents might sell their child for money among other despicable things. Children who are raised by do nothing parents are not taught about the various penalties that must be paid as a consequence of bad decisions. These are most often the children that do not experience love in the home, no hope, no tomorrow, and basically have given up on life. These children are often unable to see that there is a light at the end of the tunnel. "When you welcome even a child because of me, you welcome me. And when you welcome me, you welcome the one who sent me." (Mark 9:37 C.E.V.).

Whatever type of parent you are, remember that training your child begins with you. You are the source of knowledge, with God's help, to instruct your child in the way that will lead them to living a Godly life. Children, most likely, will one day become parents, and most parents will one day become grandparents.

Whoever coined the phrase, "It takes a village to raise a child," said something profound and true. Before that phrase was ever said, people were very much involved in the welfare of others. People watched, cared for, and were dependable when it came to others. It may have involved being the one to look after a neighbor's child, or reporting suspicious happenings that were seen occurring in your neighborhood, or parents telling other parents if, or when, they saw their child misbehaving. Then society introduced *meddling, busy body, my child can't do any wrong, snitch, and it isn't any of my business,* type of neighbors and friends.

The laws of the land began to impose penalties against parents who chose to uphold the words of the Bible, and forbid parents to exercise discipline. It was then that caring, concerned neighbors, friends, parents and strangers were frowned upon when they approached parents to tell them about the misbehavior of their children. These examples are only a fraction of the factors that have led or influenced the behavior of parents and children within the family.

The world influences other factors such as taking prayer out of the schools, allowing certain rights to individuals to engage in same-sex marriages, corruption and greed among businesses, plastering the use of sex images to sell products all over the television, just to name a few. All of these immoral things have greatly influenced the minds of people. The world will always send out the wrong message. Shamelessly, this is what children are constantly being exposed to.

As Christians, we are protected by the Most High; and we must always wear the whole armor of God. In preparation, we must be ready and rely on the power of God to fight our battles and use His wisdom to guide us to deal with these things. Your children are vulnerable to the world and therefore need to be prepared for the worldly things they will encounter. Children need to be strong to deal with the things of this world. As parents, we must help.

A good lesson for parents and children can be found in Ephesians chapter one verse five which says, "You are God's people, so do not let it be said that any of you are immoral or indecent or greedy. Do not use dirty or foolish or filthy words. Instead, say how thankful you are. Being greedy, indecent, or immoral is just another way of worshipping idols. You can be sure that people who behave in this way will never be part of the kingdom that belongs to Christ and to God" (C.E.V.).

Also, "Parents do not be hard on your children. Raise them properly. Teach them and instruct them about the Lord" (Ephesians 6:4 C.E.V.). Children remember, "Obey your father and your mother, and you will have a long and happy life" (Ephesians 6:2-3 C.E.V.).

Parents, listen, communicate, show interest, love, get involved, and have your eyes open. Most important, involve your children in a Bible studying church. At home, set aside a day each week to have family time. Family time is a way of communicating any concerns, as well as enjoying spending valuable, fun time with one another. Praying, reading from the Bible, instructing them about God and Jesus, and showing your children how much they are loved make a good foundation for a well-rounded family.

Yes, parents, be aware that you can send your children to hell by not developing a Christian environment, not preparing them for choices and not helping them develop their character.

Chapter 4
Out of the Mouths of Babes

Children are at their infancy when introduced to God and Jesus. At a very early age they know it is a good thing to have the Lord on their side by what they are taught in the home and in church. As children get older and the teachings are reinforced, they become aware about their salvation. Just as in attending school, it is a twelve year learning process with additional higher learning of attending college. In serving God, it is a life time commitment of service.

As parents, it is your responsibility to teach your children about the abundance of God's love and the rewards that are offered in being obedient. Most children are taught that there is a hell where bad, evil people go and the ones that reject God.

Children want to feel safe and protected. Children that are introduced to God and Jesus at an early age about heaven and hell are concerned. These are a few samplings from a child's point of view of hell:

London, Age 8 – I think parents are supposed to do a lot of praying and teaching their kids about God and learn how to stop the devil from getting into them.

Also, they need to learn how to praise Jesus the right way, and to remember the day Jesus died on the cross for our sins, and show love to the Lord, and pray to God every night before they go to bed and when they get up in the morning; and that's all I think it means.

Brian, Age 13 – I believe there is a hell for children. If you are at the age of accountability and you do not accept Christ as your Lord and Savior, you will go to hell. If you are not at the age of accountability you will go to heaven.

Jaylen, Age 11–I do not think there is a hell for children because there are not two of them. I think that there is one hell for everyone because I do not think He would make two separate ones for children and another hell for teens and adults.

Joshua, Age 8–I think there is not a hell for children because everybody goes to the same hell and goes to the same heaven.

Jason, Age 9 – I think there is a hell for children. Do you want to know why? I think there is because if there is a kid bad enough they should go to hell. It is God's will to know if they go to hell. People who do not believe in God will go to hell.

<u>Kristen, Age 12</u> Well, I believe that it is based on accountability. For instance, if there is a child that is two years old and dies it doesn't really have much of experience as a Christian. But a fifteen-year old would be accounted for because they are old enough to understand.

<u>Tamara, Age 8</u> – I believe there is a hell for children because we are all God's children.

Prayer is your one-on-one personal relationship with God. When we pray, we should pray for forgiveness, protection, and to give thanks for God's goodness. As parents, you should also pray for others and teach your children how to pray.

Pray for the sick and the afflicted. Pray for your loved ones, friends, and strangers if they have fallen by the wayside, to return to Christ.

Parents, teach your children to pray. Take the time to instill in them how powerful prayers are for whatever situations or conflicts they may encounter in their life. Here are some prayers children have written about their friends:

<u>Lauren, Age 6</u> - Dear Lord, I pray for my friends. I pray that they will not use bad words so they will not go to

hell. I want them to love the Lord with all their heart so they can go to heaven.

Joshua, Age 8 - Father in heaven, I pray that my friend will repent for his sins and he would be baptized.

Jason, Age 9 - If I was praying for a friend so he would not go to hell I would say: Father, in heaven, I pray that you will let my friend make the right choices and let him not get influenced. Please help him to do good and give him eternal life, and in Jesus name we pray. Amen

Jaylen, Age 11 - Father in heaven thank you for your blessings and your grace. Thank you for everything you have done God. I thank you for food, shelter, and clothing. Thank you for your kindness and your grace and everything that you have blessed me with, God. God, please forgive my friend of all he has done. All the bad he has done and for all his sins. God, I pray that he will see what all he has done and repent and not do it again. God, please let them know your Word and that you will give me the right kind of boldness to speak to him and get him in the right state of mind. In this I pray in Jesus name. Amen

Kristen, Age 12 - Dear gracious Father in heaven. I thank you for this day and thank you for waking us up this morning. But dear God I pray for one of my friends that they will accept Christ even after I have told them about Him. That they will accept You before they die. In Jesus' name I pray. Amen

Brian, Age 13 – Father, in heaven, I thank you for blessing me to speak your Word. I pray that my friend will not go to hell. I pray that he will find Jesus and that he will keep and not reject Him and that he will follow in your footsteps. Also, I will be a witness to him. In Jesus' name I pray. Amen

Children are precious. They are like diamonds in the rough. If you know anything about diamonds, you know they are cut to certain specifications. The more weight of the diamond, and the larger the caret, the more valuable the diamond becomes. This is how God and Jesus see our children, precious in their eyesight. "Children are a blessing and a gift from the Lord" (Psalms 127 vs. 3 C.E.V.). Children are very important.

As parents, you are the caregivers of your children. The responsibility of raising them properly falls on your shoulders. You must not lose sight of this. "Our human fathers correct us for a short time, and they do it as they think best. But God corrects us for our own good, because he wants us to be holy, as he is. It is never fun to be corrected. In fact, it is always painful.

But if we learn to obey by being corrected, we will do right and live at peace" (Hebrews 12 vs. 10-11 C.E.V.).

It is left up to you as parents to safeguard your children so they will know how to take care of themselves, with the help of the Lord. Times are much different now. Children are getting caught up in stuff that was once reserved for adults. The crimes today being committed by children include acts of malice, viciousness, and hate. We fail to understand why.

It is time for parents to take back control of their children and not let them be in control. Children should keep their innocence as long as possible.

Chapter 5
The Now Factor

*T*he world has turned away from what God has intended for us. God wants us to build a personal relationship with Him and truly get to know Him. "The world is in for trouble because of the way it causes people to sin. There will always be something to cause people to sin, but anyone who does this will be in for trouble" (Matthew 18 vs. 7 C.E.V.).

Greed, corruption, and selfishness are traits young people are being exposed to constantly. The world is sending a message that there is nothing wrong with seeking and acquiring material things by any means necessary. This seems to be an epidemic spreading everywhere. It seems the now factor is the force that is driving young people.

The attitude displayed by most children today is one that displays an everything has to be acted on now; quick, fast, and in a hurry. Children are often in a hurry to live their life. Most children can't wait to grow-up. They can't wait to get a job. They can't wait to get their own place. They say, "I can't wait to live my own life". As adults, most of us, at one time or another has echoed these same words while we were growing up. Children often say such things out of anger. They sometimes feel that too many restrictions are being imposed upon them. Often, they do not understand that it is out of love that their best interest is being protected. Children should be taught that the best time in their life is to be experienced by taking one day at a time.

Life is simple. Life is complicated. Life has its hardships and heartaches. It is how you choose to live your life that determines how simple, or how complicated, your life becomes. Life is a journey in experience.

There are a lot of outside factors that contribute to life altering decisions that may change your life forever. When you make poor decisions, there are consequences that follow. Everything doesn't have to be now. When you were born, you came into this world with nothing. When you leave this world, you will leave here with nothing.

The rich man in the book of Matthew, Chapter 19 wanted to know what good things he must do to get eternal life. Jesus explained it to him. The young man had kept the commandments that Jesus spoke of. When Jesus told the young man to sell all of his possessions and give them to the poor, then he would have treasure in heaven. This made the young man very sad as he had great wealth. "It is hard for a rich man to enter the kingdom of heaven. It is easier for a camel to go through the eye of a needle than for a rich man to enter the kingdom of God" (Matthew 19:21-24 C.E.V.).

Greed is a terrible disease to be consumed by. It sadly affects young and old, rich and poor. I classify this as *the have and the have not* and the *in between*. This may influence some that develop keeping up with the Jones syndrome that is passed on to your children. When you become consumed with gaining material things in life, then the one that provides for you, who has always been there for you, and will never let you down is put on the back burner, and that is God. As adults, if you forget about God, then your children adopt the same type attitude toward God.

In life there are two paths that are constantly traveled, the right path and the wrong path. You choose your path in life and you also determine how you want to live your life. You choose the right path but can still do things the wrong way, and that is when correction takes place. Choosing the wrong path is certain to always get you in trouble.

When you portray a spirit of lying, deceit, hatred, and are consumed with doing evil things, these are traits of a destructive personality. It is so sad that some children develop this type of behavior. The missing ingredient is love. Some children feel that they have to respond and act out to the point that they eventually believe they are behaving in a normal way.

As a little girl I watched a movie called the *Bad Seed*. The character appeared to be a sweet little girl until her true colors came out. She had all the bad traits of lying, deceiving, jealously, and even killed to get her own way. She set her mind upon obtaining something that didn't belong to her and killed to get it. She killed to cover up when her deadly deeds were discovered by the caretaker. Soon everything caught up with her and she self- destructed.

Some young people are consumed with obtaining things in an ill-gotten manner. Work seems not to be an option to achieve things legally. Everyone has to work for things in life. There are home invasions, car thefts, muggings, and bank robberies that have all gotten out of hand. Morality, values, honesty, and integrity have all been lost along the way. The consequences of these actions appear not to bother young people responsible for these crimes. The desire to have things at the expense of illegal acts does not only hurt our young people but it hurts their victims as well. The thought process that should tell them that they are ruining their life is not being considered.

Young people, learn how to be patient. When you have made a choice to do something wrong instead of achieving things legally, your mind, and your spirit within lets you know this. Some of the consequences you may face because of poor decisions are juvenile detention, failing grades in school, and an early grave. There is a time for everything. Do not allow Satan to take control of your life. Now is the time to get to know the Lord. Live a life that is pleasing to God. The things of this world are not all that important. It is all about getting a good education and doing something worthwhile with your life.

Remember: Put your main focus on God and He will take care of the rest, no matter what situations you face in your life. Leaving God out of your life leads to consequences you have chosen to bring upon yourself. Everything does not have to be now.

Chapter 6
Do Not Fall Victim to the Devil

There was a man who made it his mission to travel all over the countryside. On his quest, twelve others went along with him to spread the good news. He taught about the Kingdom of God and went around healing the sick. People came from everywhere after hearing about the wonderful blessings that would be bestowed and the promises of heaven. This man was Jesus.

Today there are groups that go around spreading terror and violence. They are leaders and members of all ages. Their mission is to destroy and prey on the innocent. Instead of being on the battlefield of good, they would rather rob and kill without regard to human life. The recruiting age is getting younger to let the young ones do their evil bidding. These groups of Satan followers are gang members. Threats and fear tactics are used or promises of material things are offered in exchange for becoming a gang member. Oh, if they could follow the concept of Jesus. Jesus was about love and blessings. He went around healing the sick.

Young people, please do not become a victim of the devil. The devil does not have your best interest at heart. Always strive to be good because the Lord is displeased when you do wrong. Satan is very cunning and crafty. Do not be ignorant of his devices. The devil loves trouble. It was Satan who made trouble for Eve in the Garden of Eden. He persuaded her to eat the forbidden fruit from the tree of life. Eve, in turn, convinced Adam to eat of the fruit. Satan also tried to tempt Jesus by offering Jesus all the riches in the world. Satan asked of Jesus that he bow down and worship him. Jesus sent Satan away and said "Worship the Lord your God and serve only him" (Matthew 4:10 C.E.V.).

Young people, please do not let the devil gas you up. Do not be influenced to do things that mean you no good. Reason out obstacles that come your way. Learn to pray and call upon the name of Jesus. Do not give the devil control of your life.

Once the devil has a stronghold it is hard to break those demons festering inside. Learn to control any dark emotions that may try to consume and take over your spirit. It is a constant battle of good versus evil. Good always wins in the end.

Children, you are special. When you love and respect yourself, it becomes easier to treat others with respect and compassion. Remember that Jesus Christ was about spreading love and helping others in their time of need. He did a lot of great things. The most important thing He did was to die on the cross in order to take on all of our sins.

Next, stay away from bad influences. You are only hurting yourself when you go looking for trouble. In the book of Proverbs C.E.V., chapter one, it discusses warnings against bad friends. So-called friends can get you into trouble. Eventually, you are robbed of your life. Prison and maybe even death awaits you. Seek out your parents or a responsible adult when you have a problem. Let wisdom and common sense be your guide.

Do not give anger control over your emotions. Anger is an emotion the devil feeds upon that only leads to regrets. For example, if you stab or shoot someone which results in death, that is a heavy burden to bear. The devil loves the misery you are feeling. Fighting, verbal abuse, scheming, drugs, stealing, and violence of any kind are not normal.

Pray your way out of situations that may lead you to do evil things. Stop being plastered all over the evening news. Every crime that is committed is punishable.

After we are all are judged, including Satan himself, by God, the book of Revelations states "And the devil, who deceived them, was thrown into the lake of burning sulfur, where the beast and the false prophet had been thrown. They will be tormented day and night for ever and ever" (Revelations 20:10 C.E.V.). "And I saw the dead, great and small, standing before the throne, and books were opened. Anyone whose name was not found written in the book of life was thrown into the lake of fire" (Revelations 20:12-15 C.E.V.).

Hell is a horrible place to be. Children, there is a hell where the wicked and the evil are condemned for all eternity. If you continue being a victim of the devil, you have made hell your home. Let God be the center of your life and you cannot go wrong. Focus on always doing the right thing and work toward living life in heaven for all eternity.

No one is immortal to death. Death claims us at any age. While you are here you should want the light to shine everlasting in your life. You should want to be known for your good deeds, a job well done instead of being known as someone associated with doing terrible things.

God sent Jesus as an excellent guide to imitate the kind of lives we should live. Jesus had a huge following everywhere He went spreading the good news, healing the sick, and teaching about the kingdom of God.

Children, on your quests or ventures in life, please remember to <u>always keep God first</u>. It is easy to follow the devil with all the enticements that he puts before you. But it is always better to follow and obey God and Jesus.

An eternal life in hell is permanent. It is not worth losing the best relationship you can ever achieve in this life. The blessings are bountiful. God knows that we are not immune to sin. We are forgiven when there are repentances. That is a wonderful gift from God; His son Jesus.

Chapter 7
Destruction and Hell

Sin is rampant. Life is full of temptation. The world throws out so much enticement as if it is saying, 'okay, come and get it'. Everything that appears good is not always good; for the most part, the attitude of the world says it's all about *me*. No matter who I hurt, it is about *me*. I come first. Children, you should not have that type of attitude. "We should think about others and not about ourselves" (1 Corinthians 10 vs. 24 C.E.V.).

God has a blueprint of your entire life. God sees everything. God sees good and bad. Respect and obey God! This is what life is all about. "God will judge everything we do, even what is done in secret, whether it is good or whether it is bad. Fear God, keep His commandments: for this is the whole duty of man" (Ecclesiastes 12:13-14 C.E.V.).

It is so easy to fall in the trap of following the devil but so hard in serving God. "We are tempted by our own desires that drag us off and trap us. Our desires make us sin, and when sin is finished with us, it leaves us dead" (James 1 vs. 14-15 C.E.V.).

The temptations in life can lead to destruction and hell. This maybe your downfall if you choose not to make a change. Children there are always choices. Everyone has free will. It is quite difficult and a constant battle to resist temptations that are encountered on a day to day basis. If you have a spirit of lying, of deceit, of anger, and no morals; pray and call on the Lord to help you.

There is a story that is used to illustrate the destruction of a little boy. The story is titled *Peter and the Wolf.* Peter was a young shepherd boy that was responsible to watching over a flock of sheep. One day Peter became quite bored and decided to have fun and excitement while watching the sheep. Every day he would cry 'wolf, wolf,' and the town people would stop whatever they were doing and run to his rescue. By the time the town people got there, Peter would be rolling with laughter. This went on for awhile and one day the wolf actually showed up. He cried out wolf, wolf, and this time the town people did not run to his rescue. Sad to say, Peter was swallowed up by the wolf. Peter made a choice which caused his downfall. He chose to lie and when he told the truth it was too late. His days of playing and having fun came to an end.

Make the right decision to choose life instead of death. Life is the heavenly kingdom and death is life in hell by self destruction of your actions.

Call upon the Lord to fight off temptations that can corrupt your life. Pray and seek out righteousness. Do not give in and fight off desires that will make you sin. Praise and give God all the glory. Think about all of His goodness and mercy toward you. God is good all the time.

Choosing the wrong lifestyle only destines you to destruction. It is okay to have fun but not to the extreme where it causes harm to you or others. Drinking, drugs, having sex, robbing, and killing all have bad consequences. The consequences come in many forms. Serious health problems may occur because of heavy drinking, heavy use of drugs, and even death. Unsafe sex can lead to Aids and numerous other STDs, some which can also result in death. Robbing others and committing murder leads to prison.

A spiritual death happens by not having a personal relationship with God and Jesus. When you indulge in all of these pleasures it will lead to destruction and hell.

Instead of turning to sin, remember there is another alternative. God has a gigantic heart; and He wants what's best for you. Jesus should be your best friend and not let worldly things influence your life. God loves us so much that He gave Jesus to us who made the ultimate sacrifice. The price has been paid; all you have to do is take advantage. The door for salvation is open to everyone. The love of God is so awesome that His only begotten son Jesus died on the cross for you and me to show grace and mercy and to save us from our sins.

Heaven is our eternal home so stop living a life setting you on a journey to hell. If you were to die now, are you heaven or hell bound?

Chapter 8
What Is Hell And Where Is Hell?

Hell is a subject that is not talked enough about. It is somewhat ignored. Hell is a place where the wicked go for an eternity of suffering where there is no return. It is a one-way ticket.

You should learn everything you can about the teachings of salvation. Salvation leads to being rewarded and promised a place in heaven where you will be with God and Jesus. Heaven is eternal life for the righteous but for the wicked, there is hell.

When I was a child, my take on heaven and hell was that after you die there was an elevator. If the elevator went up, then you were in heaven; but if the elevator went down, then you were in hell. Understanding the consequences did not register.

It seems today that some young people's concept of going to hell has no meaning. As parents, you must do all you can to teach your children about choices they make in life. The temptations of the world are huge and enticing. The devil is always busy gathering souls himself. Lifestyles of abuse, use of drugs, alcohol, sex, and violence has become a normal lifestyle. "The gate to destruction is wide and the road that leads there is easy to follow" (Matthew 7:13 C.E.V.).

Some children have to be burned, feel the pain as some say, "Child, I guess you do not believe fat meat is greasy." Some children feel that they are invincible to anything and have no fear that bad things can happen in life. Some children become hard when situations occur and develop a street life mentality. They live a double life-how they appear in the home and how they appear before so-called friends. They can act like an angel in the home and act like the devil himself around their friends. Situations may be made up of abandonment of a parent, children making fun of their looks and appearance. Jealousy may also occur because some children may feel their friends are living a better life than they are. Children may feel this is their hell.

Children who are raised in a Christian environment know that one thing is certain. That certainty is that we all have to die and when we die there is heaven and there is hell. Every person born will stand before God and be judged. There is no escape from the final judgment of God.

Hell is very real. You should strive to live a righteous life where the rewards are huge. The reward is eternal life in heaven. You need God's wisdom and it is only through God's wisdom that we can make the right decisions in life (Proverbs 1:20-33 C.E.V.).

Hell is a place of torment. Hell is a place reserved for the final Day of Judgment for all who are condemned, for those who choose to follow Satan's evil ways. Satan's home is a pit, a lake of fire, and burning sulfur.

Some believe hell is right here on earth. Some people believe that hell is here on earth because of the things like poverty, homelessness, and people trying to stay ahead due to the high cost of living, health crises, and money seekers. There are others who believe that hell is a state of mind and part of the English language. One meaning of hell taken from the Webster dictionary is *a sharp scolding.*

The state of mind of some people reveals that they are committing crimes, from home invasions to beating up helpless people for no reason. It is very common to hear, *go to hell, what the hell, oh hell,* and *I'll see you in hell,* etcetera.

When you tell someone *go to hell* are you condemning that person for all eternity? When you holler, *what the hell are you doing,* are you saying that person is doing the devil's work? Even when you say,

I'll see you in hell, are you condemning yourself to hell? Think about what you say before you say it. Words are powerful and should not be used frivolously.

Children, be obedient and live your life to secure your place in heaven. Live a life that is pleasing to God. Stop being foolish and getting caught up in situations that you can control. You are the captain and no one should persuade or influence you to get into stuff that would ruin your life. Sometimes you can be your own worst enemy.

Disappointments, not being loved, feelings of not belonging, loss of hope, and desperation can lead to doing unsavory things. Unsavory things are works of Satan. Satan wants you down and out. Call on the name of Jesus. He is the light. He is the way, and He will never forsake you.

Talk things out with someone and pray with someone to keep you from committing sinful acts that you will regret later. Get control of yourself instead of being out of control. Mistakes are made in life and can be corrected if you choose. Seriously think about your lifestyle when it is not a mirror image of holiness.

Hell should not be taken lightly. Hell is a place for the wicked and the nonbeliever. Do not take hell so casually. It is very serious that you get on the bound-to-heaven train. A train to hell is a one-way ticket and there is no return.

It is written in the Bible that if you reject God and do not turn away from evil, then hell is where you will go. Hell is not a make believe place. Where do you believe your eternal home is?

Chapter 9
Accountability

In the world, one is governed by the laws of the land. There are federal and state laws. In the home, you are governed by rules set by your parents. There is an even higher authority that everyone will have to come before one day; and that is God himself. There is no escape. You have to give an account for everything you do.

Training first begins in the home. Part of training is introducing God and Jesus to others. It is a process of steps that is learned in church too. Introduction to saying grace at meal times, prayer at bedtime, or reading the Bible begins in the home. Also, the love of God and Jesus should be constantly reinforced within the home and within the church. This is the start of your Christian journey throughout life.

Children, depending on your age when you decide to accept the invitation to salvation, and to accept Jesus as your personal Lord and Savior, understand obedience, and understand what it means to repent; then this is when you become accountable.

What is so wonderful is that all is forgiven when you repent through Jesus Christ. It is a life long journey of service that you constantly have to work at because of the many temptations in life. The knowledge of being surrounded by the love of Jesus and God will make your spiritual journey worthwhile.

As children, you are nurtured, loved, disciplined, taught right from wrong, and learn the consequences for bad behavior. You are made accountable for your actions. Bad behavior is punishable and not excused.

In a Christian environment, you have the love of God and Jesus. God forgives you but you should not take His forgiveness for granted. You must be humble before Him, confess your sins, and stop sinning. You are held accountable if there is neither remorse nor repentance. The payment is eternal punishment and the debt is paid in hell forever.

God cares deeply for you. Your age, background or who you are does not matter because God's reign is supreme. Most of all, He wants everyone to succeed in having eternal life through Jesus Christ. "Know ye that the Lord he is God: it is he that hath made us, and not we ourselves, we are his people, and the sheep of his pasture" (Psalms 100:3 K.J.V.).

You are held responsible when you reject and go astray from godly living. The world offers a lot of temptations. When you fall down, you can get back up. You should not be conformed to this world. This world is not your home. You have the Lord to fight your battles. "Surrender to God! Reject the devil, and he will run from you. Come near to God, and he will come near to you" (James 4:7-8 C.E.V.).

Have faith, pray, self control, obedience, and know that you can be held accountable for everything you do.

Chapter 10
Stuff

*T*here are sayings that go something like this, "When you live long enough; I thought I have seen or heard it all." Today we live in troubled times. There is so much pain, anger, violence, and not enough love. All of this is stuff many people tend to carry throughout life.

Every generation of parents brings certain challenges in raising children. It seems very simple that most parents instill morality, values, integrity, and a Christian environment in the home. Those factors have never changed in rearing children. However, somewhere life situations encountered has crossed over to children also. We all have stuff. Some of us know how to endure, know how to carry on despite what baggage we are holding on to.

Children can often be easy targets. They can easily find themselves involved in some not so pleasant situations in life without the knowledge needed to handle the consequences. Depending on their age, children do not always have the maturity required to handle problems and negative situations that they might be faced with in their young lives.

Sometimes, as young people, you may feel as if the world is stacking stuff against you and you feel there is nowhere to turn. You find yourself getting out of high school with a great grade point average then going on to college and graduating with a degree. You start to seek employment and either no one is hiring or the interviewer says the company needs someone with experience.

Some parents are failing their children when they let their personal baggage of stuff get in the way. There are a lot of good parents and caregivers that want the very best for their children. They make sure that their children are equipped to handle whatever situations they are faced with.

Examples of life situations that can affect parents and children are loss of a job, a broken marriage, bad vices such as smoking, drinking, doing drugs, and living an ungodly life.

Children may be exposed to peer pressure, gangs, robbery, fighting, having babies out of wedlock, and even taking someone else's life.

Years ago when breaking news reported a mass shooting at a school; it sent shockwaves across

America. These types of acts were usually committed by an adult. Now crimes committed by children have been taken to a whole new level. Today, jails are overcrowding with children because of poor decisions they make and the type of illegal things they get into.

Children are killing children, children are killing their parents, and parents are killing their children. The Bible says, "Parents will betray their own children, and children will turn against their parents and have them killed (Matthew 10:21 CEV).

The behavior pattern of children is most often a mirror image learned from their primary caregiver. Much of what children are exposed to has its roots inside the home, school, and can even be in the church. As adults, good examples displayed should be what children see. When children come into this world, we do not know if that child will be a doctor, lawyer, or murderer. Children have a blank slate and the lives they lead are patterned after their parents. You only hope for the best from your children.

You can always call upon a source any time of the day or night that is very dependable. He has a great track

record. He has been here from the very beginning, and He will be here until the very end of time. There are some people who refuse to acknowledge that they have problems and face trials, but no matter where you come from, or where you have been, you can leave your problems to God. God is so awesome and He can fix any problem you face.

Children can only learn how to communicate, learn from their mistakes, and be able to depend on their parents if parents exemplify good habits for them to follow.

Chapter 11
Encourage Yourself

Encouraging yourself is building self-confidence within. Encouraging yourself means having self-esteem. Encouraging yourself also means having a positive outlook. Encouraging yourself is not allowing anyone to turn you around. All of these are weapons you can use against the enemy. The enemy's agenda is to defeat you with words that hurt, lower your self esteem, and inflict pain.

Children, always make a habit of encouraging yourself so that you will be ready to stand against whatever comes at you in the way of the enemy.

If you allow pain and the anger to settle inside of you, it can destroy your life. Do not be a victim of the blame game syndrome and let it take over your life. Encourage yourself to overcome and know that God protects His own. You can only be hurt if you allow it to happen. When bad stuff happens, look at the positive side of things instead of the negative side. Stuff or situations you bring upon yourself is your mess. Only you can stop it.

You feel as if you want to throw in the towel and say the heck with all of this. But I come to tell you that you have to encourage yourself. Acts 11:23 tells us to be encouraged and stay true to the Lord with all our hearts. Sometimes you have to speak a word to yourself, anointing yourself with oil and go before the Lord saying "Lord, I put my faith and trust in you, please give me the strength to endure." Matthew 17:20 says: "If you have faith as small as a mustard seed, you can say to this mountain, 'Move from here to there' and it will move. Nothing will be impossible for you."

When you carry around emotional baggage, examine yourself and make a change for the best. Love, joy, kindness, and helping others by doing good deeds can bring a feeling of goodness within.

Harboring and feeling bad only brings you down and may even resort to you doing bad things. Make every day your best day. Depending on your age, begin to make a practice of thanking God for looking after you in the good times as well as the bad times.

Start giving God thanks for everything. Life is not a bed of roses. Life is not always kind. You will encounter haters, jealousy, and mean-spirited people but do not be any of those types of people. Grow up and become like Jesus who stands for love. It is God who loves us best. He sent Jesus to take on our sins for us to repent. With both of them in your corner, you cannot go wrong.

There is a song that goes like this: *It's me, O, Lord standing in the need of prayer. Not my brother, not my sister, but it's me O, Lord standing in the need of prayer.*

Remember: You cannot piggy back off anyone to receive Christ in your life. You have to be the one to make the decision for yourself. When you choose to do nothing, you have still made a choice.

You will have difficult situations that you face in life. You can take comfort that life will be so much easier to use God and Jesus as a place of refuge to seek out in your time of need. When God is in your life there is no room for ill feelings.

Surround yourself with what you love in life such as family, hobbies, good relationships, and Jesus.

Again, make everyday your best day. Quit tripping over things that you cannot control. Incorporate a *Yes I Can* attitude and make life simple instead of complicated. Yes, I can face whatever comes my way, and yes I can with the help of my God. Nothing can hurt me. Never worry about the opinions of others.

There is only one opinion that truly matters and that is God's opinion.

It was not easy for Jesus when He walked here on earth. He was determined, persistent, and conquered the obstacles and challenges that were presented. He taught a lot of life lessons-the parables you find presented as examples when he ministered. Jesus stayed encouraged despite the hardships. He was put on trial because He was misunderstood by some that didn't want to believe or accept Him as the son of God. Jesus stayed encouraged. He was on a mission to do His father's work.

Children, be encouraged for the difficulties and challenges as Jesus met until He was crucified on the cross. Life is compiled of tests and tribulations we face. At the end, there is victory through Jesus Christ and because He lived; we can face tomorrow. We can face anyone or anything.

Let Jesus be the one to lead you and guide you. Never be associated with nonbelievers and Satan. Never give up the good fight of living a godly life.

Remember. You are in God's care and because Jesus lives, you can stay encouraged.

Chapter 12
Nice Parents
Have Difficult Children Too

Married and single families that have a Christian environment have difficult children also. There are many factors that contribute to raising children in a world full of greed, hate, and violence. Time away from home spent working, not knowing your children's friends, not monitoring what your children watch on TV, and not giving them enough responsibilities. All of these things have an impact on children.

Idle time and boredom can lead to children doing things that get them in trouble. I'm sure you've heard "an idle mind is the devil's workshop." This is actually a true statement. When children do not have enough things to keep them busy doing constructive things, trouble, with a capital **T** follows.

Depending on the age, children may experiment with smoking, drinking, experimenting with drugs, having sex, shoplifting, just to name a few of hundreds of things that lead to destruction. Though the children are raised properly, with values, Christian morals and taught life lessons in the home, sometimes they are still drawn to experience the hard knocks of life. They go in search for something that appeals to them and offers what they believe is exciting. It's like another saying, "the grass is greener on the other side." After the appeal has worn off and the disappointments or error of their ways, they return home. That is when they may hopefully understand that "the grass is not always greener on the other side of the fence."

In Luke Chapter fifteen starting at verse eleven, Jesus tells the parable of two sons. The father divides the property between his two sons. The younger son is determined to leave home and venture out into a foreign country and start having a good time. He has so much fun that soon all of his inheritance is spent. The storm this son went through by messing off all of his inheritance until he becomes pennilessness continues as he finds himself having to go to work in a strange land. He finds himself working for someone cleaning up behind the hogs. He is so hungry and desperate that he begins to eat right along with the pigs! It is at this point in his life that the son realizes that he has made a mess of his life. He soon wises up and decides to return where even his father's servants eat better and live better than he is living. He begins to realize that at home he can at least eat with the servants and still live better than the life he lives among the pigs. The son returns to the home of his father. He plans to let his father know that he has sinned against God in heaven and his father, and that he isn't good enough to be his son.

The father sees his son approaching and quickly runs to him and gives him hugs and kisses. He is so happy to see his son return home, that he orders the servants to bring the best clothes, a ring, sandals, and prepare the best calf for his son to eat.

The other son had been working out in the fields, hears music and sees dancing when he approaches the house. When the older son is told the reason for the celebration, he becomes so angry that he refuses to go inside of his father's house. His father comes out and begs his beloved son to come inside, but the son complains about how hard he works and how obedient he is, yet he has not been given even a goat to entertain his friends. The older son is angry because he knows his brother left home and wasted all of his inheritance on frivolous living. The father lovingly reminds his older son that everything he has is his. He explains to him that he is happy because his younger son who was dead has returned home and now he is found. The older son failed to realize that all of the years that he remained with his father that he had access to everything.

When a child goes astray, rebels and chooses a life totally different from what godly parents have instilled in that child, unfortunately no amount of discipline, lecturing, or explaining the consequences seems to matter. When this occurs, there is a feeling of helplessness that consumes parents. This is especially true when parents have to work and find it almost impossible to keep tabs on that child who is acting out in destructive ways.

There are no easy answers. Some children are needier than other siblings in the household. Spending extra time, having a special outing, counseling, and prayer are a few solutions. God always has the answers.

Continue to instill moral training and discipline in your children. Never give up on your children. Parents, good examples displayed consistently before your child(ren) may help a difficult child respond back positively to their Christian environment.

Chapter 13
Nice Children
Have Difficult Parents Too

The relationship developed between the parent and the child is perception from either party. Part of the problem may be communication. The parent dictates the standards and sets the rules in the home. The child may feel the parent doesn't understand where they are coming from. To be able to communicate effectively, parents need to take the time to clearly define the meaning when talking and explaining things to children.

One parent may say or ask a child, for example, will you watch the potatoes in the oven, and turn them over in about fifteen minutes? What does *turn the potatoes* mean to a child who is say thirteen years of age or so? An adult perceives that *turn the potatoes* means flipping the potatoes over. To the child, it may be perceived as just turning the pan of potatoes around. The parent may get upset when actually they should not because it is about perception of how the parent sees things as opposed to how the child sees things. The child feels the parent is too harsh, thus a communication breakdown.

Children are sensitive and some do wear their heart on their sleeve. The amount and manner of temperament displayed by parents can make children feel they have difficult parents.

Some parents' natural way of communication is hollering, being short tempered, and everything appears to get on their nerves. As adults, if you can sense when other adults are short tempered and easily upset, then understand that children are in tune with how they see their parents too.

Parents can be consumed with their own personal issues and roles seem to become reverse between the parent and the child. When this occurs, some children grow up very fast because of the responsibilities the child has undertaken.

Life issues some adults incur may be due to the death of a loved one, like a spouse, and the parent does not know how to cope with the magnitude of that loss. It may be one, or both, parents that have addictions to drugs or alcohol and have been wearing a mask pretending all is well. Children can sense emotional stress in their parents.

Parents, you must understand that just like you can become stressed, your child can become stressed too.

Stress is a factor where the adult cannot manage in a positive way. Stress is dangerous in an adult and a child. Stress can lead to serious health issues such as a stroke, heart attack, or a mental breakdown. Stress in children can lead to withdrawal, rebellion and sadly, suicide. So, parents, remember to seek help from a counselor, your church, physician or a professional who can help you learn how to manage stress.

Unsolved adult problems can have a negative impact on children. The parent may inflict a sense of guilt or make the child feel it is their fault for whatever has occurred. The child goes into parental mode to make sure things in the household are running fine as not to cause any conflicts. This is another unhealthy position for a child. Parents need to be parents so that children can be allowed to be children.

Maybe at one point, the child knew there was a great love by their primary caregiver and then one day the situation in the home changed. Children may pretend that there is nothing wrong. They want everything to appear normal. They want to feel secure in their own surroundings.

Children may feel that if everything appears normal then the parent may return to being the parent they were before everything backfired in the family. They may have developed a false blanket that is only temporary until things go back as before.

I cannot stress enough that parents should remain in their given roles and be parents. No matter how mature you want to believe your child is, a child lacks the maturity needed to be a parent; and they shouldn't have to be placed in such a position.

Children may also set themselves up in a fantasy world; hoping and believing they can fix things because of the deep love that child has for their parents.

Depression can set in for all involved—parents and children. This is the time to turn to the Lord because He is the only one who has the solutions to any problems the family faces.

Children, when you feel that there is a language gap between you and your parents, pray to God to give you the words to say and ask God to show you how to approach your parents so you can talk to them about your feelings. There is none between God. He really understands. He wants you to come to Him and depend on Him.

Children, pray for your parent or parents as they may have taught you. God hears even the simplest of prayers. God can make everything right. "I praise you, Lord for being my guide. Even in the darkest night, your teachings fill my mind. I will always look to you, as you stand beside me and protect me from fear. With all my heart, I will celebrate, and I can safely rest" (Psalms 16:7-9 CEV).

Chapter 14
Everybody Wants To Be Loved

"God loves you and has chosen you as his own special people". "Love is more important than anything else. It is what ties everything completely together" (Colossians Chapter 3:12, 14 C.E.V.).

Throughout all generations, God has been there. "God is! He is "Alpha and Omega, the beginning and the end, the first and the last," (Revelations 22:13 KJV). He is "The same yesterday, and today, and forever" (Hebrews 13:8 KJV). God's love is overflowing. The magnitude of His love is so powerful. God's love is unconditional. He has demonstrated it repeatedly. God only asks that you get close and personal with Him through prayer and by studying His word, which is The Bible. God wants you to solely depend on Him.

In life, stuff happens. One has storms. Life situations happen and it can cause bitterness to show its ugly self. When bad things happen, that is when all the teachings from your upbringing and relying on wisdom are needed to guide you through the storm.

Remember. A storm you go through is only temporary. You can fight your way through difficult situations and not resort or use excuses to do terrible things. Call upon the Lord and Jesus like you call your momma or daddy. "Trust in the Lord with all thine heart, and lean not unto thine own understanding. In all thy ways acknowledge him, and he shall direct thy paths". (Proverbs 3:5-6 KJV).

Emotional scars are often the worst to deal with. This is a strong area that affects a lot of children. Life can be cruel. Children, whatever emotional scars you experience, whether someone called you fat, ugly, talks about you, teases you, or even if you have parents that do these types of things, please stand strong. Try to remember that God will bring you through. It may be hard because words do hurt. The thing is you do not have to deal with emotional scars alone. Do not let anger set in nor have a pity party. You are better than that when you have God on your side. God will be with you always. When you do good things blessings will follow. It will be like a heavy down pour by being obedient to the word of God.

Understanding the magnitude of His greatness and the love He has for you should be your primary focus in life. It is now the time that you seek Him and let God consume your life. God should be like a contagious disease where there is no cure. Whatever situations you face that you cannot handle, remember God will not fail in coming to your rescue. You should always encourage ourselves with the knowledge there is nothing too hard for God to solve.

Happiness and love are the keys to living a righteous life. Treat everyone with love in your heart. You will encounter people that will not set right with your spirit but learn to be tolerant, accept them for who they are. That doesn't mean that you have to hang out with that person, but it does mean that you should not be cruel or mean to that person.

Pray and learn to lean more on Jesus. You have to be willing and have the heart to build good relationships. Look at the goodness that surrounds you and no matter how things seem, do not complicate a situation by substituting false love to make yourself feel better. Using drugs, drinking alcohol, having sex, or joining a gang can never replace the feeling that God can give you inside.

You are more worthy than the things that the enemy tries to use to trick you. The only thing you need is the love of God, and He has already promised that He will never leave you or forsake you. His love is so great and if you understand this, then when problems arise as they often do, you will know that you have someone to turn to rather than turning to the wrong place, or doing the wrong thing.

There is a song I ran across in the *Women of Colors Study Bible*. The song is titled, *'Tis Love That Makes Us Happy*. It was written many years ago (in 1892) by F. E. Belden. I'd like to share the words of this song with you.

God is love; we're His little children. God is love; we would be like Him. "Tis love that makes us happy, "Tis love that smooths the way, it helps us mind, it makes us kind, to others every day.

Chapter 15
Turning Things Around

It is not an easy task to turn things around. There are so many temptations in life that children are being exposed to. It is a long, hard road that you constantly have to work at. Our children are what we make them. Their character is shaped from instructing them by standards set through examples and training. Parents, you must continue to instruct your children in the teachings of a Christian life. This cannot be stressed enough. It depends on your lifestyle as parents.

Some parents who fail their children may not have a relationship with God. Therefore, some children will not have the knowledge of the consequences of what is right and wrong. But it is never too late. Anyone can have a new start, a new beginning. "Whether you turn to the right or to the left, your ears will hear a voice behind you saying, "This is the way, walk in it" (Isaiah 30:21 NIV).

It is a daily walk with Jesus to grow spiritually. You need more of God's power to deal with obstacles and road blocks that come your way. The devil is always busy. Every day the devil is recruiting to build his domain. The devil preys on the weak and reels them in with enticements to trap his victims.

It does not have to be that way. Life itself can be a struggle and there is always a better solution. If you are coping with things like peer pressure, addictions, disobedience, and living an unholy life, you can have God. When you look up at the sky, as far as the sky stretches in width, God is able to carry all your burdens on His shoulders. There is nothing too hard for God to solve.

Parents, so many of your children are being lost to violence. Many of them are having children at an early age, experimenting with drugs and alcohol, joining gangs, and having anger management issues. Satan is really enjoying all of this because he gets a kick out of all the souls he will be collecting. He wants to destroy the relationship that parents should have with their children.

Children, you do not have to condemn yourself to hell. God is about salvation and redemption through His son Jesus who died and shed His blood for your sins. Children, take stock of your life. Examine what you want for yourself in life. We are all living in troubled times. Your parents' guidance and God's wisdom will follow you all the days of your life. It all depends on you.

God's plan for us that everyone be saved. We are all sinners. When we act out and not living a life pleasing to God, we are living in sin. God has been here for us but we as His children have left Him. God's plan is for us to rely on Him, trust in Him, and believe whole heartedly that Jesus died on the cross to save us from our sins. "For God so loved the world that He gave His only begotten Son, that whosoever believeth in Him should not perish, but have everlasting life". (John 3:16 KJV).

When you confess your sins, repent for your wrong doings and turn to God; you are in good fellowship with Him. You want your relationship to be strengthened through your faith. You want to be part of His glorious kingdom for all eternity. That is the greatest reward, greater than winning a mega lottery. The world is only a temporary place until you go to your permanent home. While you are here, you should live everyday as if it is your last days.

Yes, children make everyday count. Be grateful. Love yourself and others. Be full of joy, considerate of others, and always keep Jesus in your life. Peace and contentment will be with you.

Children, adopt the word **change** in your way of thinking. Practice forgiveness, rid yourself of hate, and focus on being kind to others, including yourself. Also, rid yourself of critical tendencies. Do not hang on to grudges, make up to those you have wronged. Love with a capital L-O-V-E stamped into your heart. You will make mistakes growing up. None of us is perfect. The choices made and the road travelled is an uphill battle.

Children, you will run into twist and turns. You will run into bumps along the way in this life. At every obstacle encountered there is a crossroad that you have to decide in life. Never be persuaded or tempted by situations that you know are wrong.

Your parents have instilled in you wisdom along with the knowledge of God and Jesus that you can depend on. Prayer, studying the word of God, and having a one on one conversation with Jesus in problems you face are tools that you can use every day. These are the weapons that you have at your disposal to fight the enemy.

Remember: The race is won when the enemy cannot harm you. Being steadfast and obedient in the spirit of the Lord and Jesus is what it's all about.

Scripture References

Proverbs 22:6–Train up a child in the way he should go and when he is old he will not depart from it.

Proverbs 23:13-14–Do not fail to correct your children. You won't kill them by being firm and it may even save their lives.

Proverbs 20:7–Good people live right and God bless the children who follow their example.

Proverbs 22:15–All children are foolish, but firm correction will make them change.

Ephesians 6:2-4–Raise them properly. Teach them and instruct them about the Lord.

Hebrews 12:7-8–Be patient when you are being corrected! This is how God treats his children. Do not all parents correct their children? God corrects all of his children, and if he doesn't correct you, then you do not really belong to him.

Proverbs 13:24–If you love your children, you will correct them, if you do not love them, you will not correct them.

Proverbs 24:10–Do not give up and be helpless in times of trouble.

James 1:4-5–But you must learn to endure everything, so that you will be completely mature and not lacking in anything. If any of you need wisdom, you should ask God, and it will be given to you. God is generous and will not correct you for asking.

Mark 9:37–When you welcome even a child because of me, you welcome me. And when you welcome me, you welcome the one who sent me.

Ephesians 5:1-5–You are God's people, so do not let it be said that any of you are immoral or indecent or greedy. Do not use dirty or foolish or filthy words. Instead, say how thankful you are. Being greedy, indecent, or immoral is just another way of worshipping idols. You can be sure that people who behave in this way will never be part of the kingdom that belongs to Christ and to God.

Ephesians 6:4–Parents do not be hard on your children. Raise them properly. Teach them and instruct them about the Lord.

Ephesians 6:2-3–Obey your father and your mother, and you will have a long and happy life.

Psalms 127:3–Children are a blessing and a gift from the Lord.

Hebrews 12:10-11–Our human fathers correct us for a short time, and they do it as they think best. But God corrects us for our own good, because he wants us to be holy, as he is. It is never fun to be corrected. In fact, it is always painful. But if we learn to obey by being corrected, we will do right and live at peace.

Matthew 18:7–The world is in for trouble because of the way it causes people to sin. There will always be something to cause people to sin, but anyone who does this will be in for trouble.

Matthew 19:21-24–is a parable of a wealthy young man seeking the kingdom of heaven.

Matthew 4:10–Worship the Lord your God and serve only him.

Proverbs 1–Discusses warnings against bad friends.

1 Corinthians 10:24–We should think about others and not about ourselves.

Ecclesiastes 12:13-14–Respect and obey God! This is what life is all about. God will judge everything we do, even what is done in secret, whether good or bad.

Fear God, keep his commandments: for this is the whole duty of man.

James 1:14-15–We are tempted by our own desires that drag us off and trap us. Our desires make us sin, and when sin is finished with us, it leaves us dead.

Matthew 7:13–The gate to destruction is wide and the road that leads there is easy to follow.

Proverbs 1:20-33–You need God's wisdom and it is only through God's wisdom that we can make the right decisions in life.

Psalms 100:3–Know ye that the Lord he is God: it is he that hath made us, and not we ourselves, we are his people, and the sheep of his pasture.

James 4:7-8–Surrender to God! Reject the devil, and he will run from you. Come near to God, and he will come near to you.

Matthew 10:32-33-Whosoever therefore shall confess me before men, him will I confess also before my Father which is in heaven. But whosoever shall deny me before men, him will I also deny before my Father which is in heaven.

Matthew 10:21–Parents will betray their own children, and children will turn against their parents and have them killed.

Acts 11:23-Lord I put my faith and trust in you, please give me the strength to endure.

Matthew 17:20-If you have faith as small as a mustard seed, you can say to this mountain, Move from here to there and it will move.

Psalm 16:7-9-I praise you, Lord, for being my guide. Even in the darkest night, your teachings fill me mind. I will always look to you, as you stand beside me and protect me from fear.

Luke 15:11-31–Discusses the parable of the two sons.

Colossians 3:12, 14–God loves you and has chosen you as his own special people. Love is more important than anything else. It is what ties everything completely together.

Revelations 22:13–God is! He is Alpha and Omega, the beginning and the end, the first and the last.

Hebrews 13:8–He is the same yesterday, and today, and forever.

Proverbs 3:5-6–Trust in the Lord with all thine heart, and lean not unto thine own understanding. In all thy ways acknowledge him, and he shall direct thy paths.

Isaiah 30:21–Whether you turn to the right or to the left, your ears will hear a voice behind you saying, This is the way, walk in it.

John 3:16-For God so loved the world, that he gave his only begotten Son, that whosoever believeth in him would not perish, but have everlasting life.

Revelations 20:10 C.E.V.-And I saw the dead, great and small, standing before the throne, and books were opened.

Revelations 20:12-15 C.E.V.-Anyone whose name was not found written in the book of life was thrown into the lake of fire."

Discussion Questions

As parents, do you believe you can send your child(ren) to hell?

Do you believe lifestyle plays a role in raising well-rounded children? If so, how? If not, why not.

Do you believe certain parental tools are needed to raise well-equipped children? If so, what type of parental tools?

What type of parent are you? Why?
    a. Blinded by Love Parent
    b. Protective Parent
    c. Do Nothing Parent
    d. Do Right Parents Parent

Discuss ways to create family time.

What do you think can be done to improve communication between parent/child?

What do you think can be done to improve communication between parent/child?
Child/parent?

How do you as a parent, deal with emotional scars of your children?

How should you as a parent deal with emotional scars so it will not affect your children?

How do you teach your children to be thankful?

How do you show thanks as a parent?

How do you show thanks to others as a child?

How do you teach children to how to love? Can children teach parents how to love?

Discuss what life lessons you can impart on your children? What life lessons can your children impart to parents?

Index of Definitions

Accountable – required to render account, answerable.

Angry – feeling, extreme emotion due to hurt feelings, hostile.

Attitude – a mood or feeling, a way of thinking.

Authority – a person who runs something or controls it.

Behavior – manner of acting or bearing oneself, conduct.

Character – the moral makeup of a person.

Communication – exchange of information between people.

Consistent – sticking to the same principles, the same throughout.

Destruction – the act of tearing down, causing harm or damage.

Discipline – strict training to teach self-control.

Emotion – feelings, passion, excitement.

Eternal – endless, infinite, forever.

Family – a parent or parents and children.

God – a being conceived as the perfect, omnipotent, ruler of the universe.

Hate – to dislike, detesting.

Heaven – the home of God, where the saved go to live after death.

Hell – a place where Satan lives, and where the wicked go when they die.

Jesus – the son of God and the Messiah.

Listen – to pay attention to what someone is saying.

Love – a very strong warm feeling or deep concern for someone, commitment.

Mistake – an error.

Moral – ethical, honest, concerned with right conduct.

Obedient – willing to do what one is told to do.

Obligation – the binding power of a promise.

Obstacles – something that stands in the way.

Patience – the act of waiting calmly for someone or something.

Repetition – doing or saying something over and over.

Relationship – the association between things, the affect one thing has on another.

Right – what is fair and good.

Rules – a law, a guide for conduct or procedure.

Satan – devil, fallen angel

Scars – to cause deep unforgettable pain.

Sin – an act that harms someone, to violate a moral principle.

Value – what something is worth.

Wisdom – learning and the capacity to use it.

About the Author

*J*acquelyn D. Currie is a mother of three and grandmother of seven who loves the Lord with all of her heart. She resides in the South where she spends most of her time enjoying her grandchildren. She is living her dream by pursuing a career in writing. *Is There A Hell For Children?* is her first book as a published author. Currie has other literary works in progress, including a children's series.

A Special Invitation

But Jesus called them unto me, and said, Suffer little children to come unto me, and forbid them not; for of such is the kingdom of God (Luke 18:16 – KJV).

The only assured way to escape hell is to receive Jesus Christ as your personal Lord and Savior. Christ is the solid foundation for families. If you want to give your children the best path in life, this foundation far exceeds any career path or personal goals.

I invite you to receive Jesus Christ as your Lord and Savior. If you want that path that leads to eternal life here is how to receive it:

1. **Admit** you are a sinner and you have fallen short of the glory of God.

2. **Repent** of your sins. Turn from your ways and turn to Jesus.

3. **Confess** with your mouth and believe in your heart that Jesus is Lord.

4. **Receive** baptism as a confirmation of your faith.

Book Order Form

Quantity	Description	Cost	Total
	Is There A Hell For Children?	$12.95	

BOOK SHIPPING INFORMATION
PRINT PLEASE

Name_____

Address_____

_____

City_____

State/ Zip_____

Email _____

Phone (+ area code)_____

Money orders or cashier's checks only	Total
Subtotal	
S&H	
Taxes (If applicable)	
Total amount enclosed	

Make checks, money orders and cashiers' checks
payable to Jacquelyn D. Currie
mail to
Jacquelyn D. Currie
c/o Delo publishing
541 Moline Road
Memphis, TN 38109

Thank You for Your Support

NOTES

To contact author Jacquelyn D. Currie

about arranging speaking engagements,
book events, conferences and more
Email: hdelo1980@yahoo.com
Website: www.jacquelyndcurrie.com

Made in the USA
Charleston, SC
24 September 2011